Mental Fitness Puzzles

A LATERAL THINKING APPROACH

Kyle Hendrickson
Julie Hendrickson
Matt Kenneke
Danny Hendrickson

Illustrated by Myron Miller

Sterling Publishing Co., Inc.
New York

DEDICATION
To our parents, for teaching us the value
of independent thought

ACKNOWLEDGEMENTS

The authors would like to thank all those family members
whose insight and encouragement has contributed so much
to the production of this book. We are especially indebted to
Albert Kenneke, Joan Kenneke, Scott Hendrickson, Charlotte
Hendrickson and Verlon Hendrickson.

Library of Congress Cataloging-in-Publication Data
Mental fitness puzzles : a lateral thinking approach / Kyle
   Hendrickson...[et al.]; illustrated by Myron Miller.
      p.   cm.
   Includes index.
   ISBN 0-8069-0899-8
   1. Puzzles. 2. Lateral thinking. I. Hendrickson, Kyle.
II. Miller, Myron, 1948-
GV1493.M37   1998
793.73–dc21   98-14801
                              CIP

10 9 8 7 6 5 4 3 2 1

Published by Sterling Publishing Company, Inc.
387 Park Avenue South, New York, N.Y. 10016
© 1998 by Matthew Kenneke, Daniel Hendrickson,
Julie Hendrickson, and Kyle Hendrickson
Distributed in Canada by Sterling Publishing
% Canadian Manda Group, One Atlantic Avenue, Suite 105
Toronto, Ontario, Canada M6K 3E7
Distributed in Great Britain and Europe by Cassell PLC
Wellington House, 125 Strand, London WC2R 0BB, England
Distributed in Australia by Capricorn Link (Australia) Pty Ltd.
P.O. Box 6651, Baulkham Hills, Business Centre,
NSW 2153, Australia
Manufactured in the United States of America
All rights reserved

Sterling ISBN 0-8069-0899-8

CONTENTS

INTRODUCTION

For veterans of lateral thinking puzzles this book needs no introduction, and our only wish would be that we have created a book which will give you many hours of enjoyment. For the neophyte, this short introduction should help to explain what lateral thinking puzzles are about and offers our suggestions as to how you might best enjoy them.

Lateral thinking is the process of freeing your mind of preconceptions and allowing yourself to approach a problem in an unconventional way.

The puzzles given here can be worked on "solo," or one-on-one, or in a small group—whereby one person knows the answer and the others try to guess. The clues section is especially helpful when working alone, as it allows the solver to validate guesses without peeking at the answer.

In working lateral thinking puzzles, there is often no set limit on the number of questions that can be asked toward finding the given solution, but responses are always confined to either "Yes," "No," or "Irrelevant." We realize that some of the puzzles will have more than one plausible answer, but suggest that the solver be encouraged to determine the solution we have provided.

Whether you enjoy these puzzles propped up in bed, sitting around the campfire, traveling on a long trip, or entertaining guests in your living room, we hope your adventure into the world of lateral thinking is both challenging and enlightening.

PUZZLES

A FIRE ESCAPE

Nicole awakes to the smell of smoke. Although she realizes the danger in her situation, she makes no attempt to leave the building where she has been sleeping. Why?

Clues: 38 / Answer: 83

THE UNSUCCESSFUL SUICIDE

Feeling suicidal, a man tries to kill himself by jumping off a high-rise building. He miraculously survives the fall. Why don't the police charge him with attempted suicide?

Clues: 38 / Answer: 93

Theft in a Pub

J.P. visits his favorite local pub. While coming back from the restroom he sees a stranger take his wallet from his jacket, which he had left draped over his chair. J.P. watches the thief spend the money. Can you explain this passive response?

CLUES: 39 / ANSWER: 93

To Tell a Mockingbird

Christopher learns about a terrible crime that has been committed by John and Bob. He has known both of these men for many years and cares for them equally. Why, then, does he only report John to the authorities and not Bob?

CLUES: 39–40 / ANSWER: 93.

More Than He Bargained For

One day, while he is window shopping, Bert is suddenly aware that his retirement nest egg is gone. Can you explain how Bert came to this realization?

CLUES: 40 / ANSWER: 87

The Frustrated Futures Trader

Every day, on his drive to work in downtown Manhattan from his home in New Jersey, Joe is frustrated by his lack of foresight. Why?

CLUES: 41 / ANSWER: 83

An Untimely Death

Cal loves his pet, Roscoe, very much. In fact, he even brings Roscoe to work with him every day. After returning from lunch one day, Cal and his co-workers were very alarmed to find Roscoe dead. Can you explain the panic which followed their discovery?

CLUES: 41 / ANSWER: 93

The Long Road Ahead

Bubba sets out on a hazardous journey. Although his destination is in sight the entire time, he has to travel 400 miles in order to reach his destination. Can you explain the circumstances surrounding this event?

CLUES: 41 / ANSWER: 85

The Prison Break

Jim develops an elaborate plan to escape from prison. After successfully escaping, Jim makes a mocking phone call to the prison authorities. He reveals that he is only a few miles away at a local tavern frequented by many off-duty prison guards. The authorities are dismayed by this news, yet make no attempt to take him back into custody. Can you explain their unusual reaction?

CLUES: 42 / ANSWER: 89

Wood That I Could

Tom is stranded on a island. Although he has firewood and matches, he spends several nights shivering and cold. On the tenth night it begins to rain and Tom decides to light a fire. What's going on here?

CLUES: 42 / ANSWER: 94

A SHOOTING AT MIDNIGHT

A man walks into his backyard in the middle of the night and fires a gun. Due to his strange behavior he never sees another sunrise. (No, he didn't kill himself!) Can you explain this odd occurrence?

CLUES: 42 / ANSWER: 91

EXECUTION AT DAWN

After a short court-martial, General Gordo selects seven of his best marksmen to serve on a firing squad. They fire on the condemned man at point-blank range, yet only six bullets are found in his body. Why?

CLUES: 43 / ANSWER: 81

9

The Leaky Boat

Al is a well-known boat builder. He spends nearly a year hand-crafting a boat from the finest timber available. When he finally launches his boat it sinks within a few minutes. Satisfied, he returns home. Can you explain the man's reaction?

CLUES: 43 / ANSWER: 85

Wonder Woman

A woman is at work. She is asked to move a two-ton piece of equipment. Although no one assists her and there are no mechanical aids available, she easily completes the task. How does she comply with this seemingly impossible request?

CLUES: 43 / ANSWER: 94

By the Time I Get to Phoenix

One day Nick boasted to his friend, Frank, that he had once driven an automobile from coast to coast in less than twenty-four hours. Naturally, Frank realizes that Nick has finally stretched the truth to the breaking point. Frank offers his boastful buddy five thousand dollars if Nick can duplicate his miraculous driving feat. Although it pained him greatly to do so, Frank conceded defeat as soon as Nick explained how it could be done. What was Nick's explanation?

CLUES: 44 / ANSWER: 78

Dead Men Tell No Tales

A search party was looking for a man. They finally found him lying in a field covered in blood. Later that day, the coroner revealed that the man had been shot twice. Without any other physical evidence, the police quickly arrested the murderer. How were the police able to ascertain the identity of the criminal?

CLUES: 44 / ANSWER: 79–80

Out of Bounds

In November of 1952 a momentous football game took place between two fierce rivals. With two minutes to go in the fourth quarter, a field goal was kicked to tie the score at 13–13. Despite the loud protests of the players and spectators, the game was declared a draw, and it was not completed or replayed. Why would the game officials make such a dissatisfying and unpopular ruling?

CLUES: 44 / ANSWER: 88

Swimming with the Fishes

A man was fishing on a large lake when he suddenly fell in. Although the man was an accomplished swimmer and was only a few yards away from shore, he eventually drowned. Why did this happen?

CLUES: 45 / ANSWER: 92

The Domino Effect

Charlotte picks up a teaspoon of sugar using only one finger. How?

CLUES: 45 / ANSWER: 80

The Runaway

Alex is at a sporting event, minding his own business and, in fact, in deep concentration. Suddenly, right in front of him, a man appears, takes something from him, and quickly runs off. Instead of trying to catch the man and retrieve the item, Alex simply stands passively and watches as he runs away. Why?

CLUES: 46 / ANSWER: 90

Shortchanged

Minnie receives a sure-fire gambling tip that would put her on Easy Street. She has several dollars' worth of change in her pocket and finds a working pay phone to call her bookie. Why, then, does she lose out on her one and only chance at making the "big score"?

CLUES: 46 / ANSWER: 91

MONEY TROUBLES

A man is charged with a crime and placed in jail. His bond is set at one hundred thousand dollars. Although he desperately wants to leave and could easily get the money, he decides to remain in jail. Why?

CLUES: 47 / ANSWER: 86

PHOTO FINISHED

Ben is accused of murder. He claimed that at the time the murder had taken place, he was on vacation in the South Pacific. To back up his alibi he provided the police with videotapes of his week-long vacation. Why, then, was he eventually convicted of the crime?

CLUES: 47 / ANSWER: 89

KEEP ON TRUCKIN'

Lewis attends the International Convention of Truckers. While in the noisy convention hall he sees a group of men on the far side of the room. He does not recognize any of them. Without hearing them speak or seeing anything distinctive about their wardrobe, Lewis announces to his colleagues: "There's the group from Australia. I think I'll go over and introduce myself." How did he come to his rapid and accurate conclusion?

CLUES: 47–48/ ANSWER: 84

MR. GRAY'S ANATOMY

Mr. Gray's life was going perfectly. He was healthy, successful, and had a beautiful family. Therefore his parents were shocked when he made a very strange request. Mr. Gray asked that his head be cut off. Why did he make this bizarre request?

CLUES: 48 / ANSWER: 87

POTTED PLANTS

When Fred decided to grow a large quantity of marijuana on his remote farm, he thought he had the perfect plan. He would grow the plants in a large barn using artificial lights. No one ever visited him and he was the only person involved in the operation. So it was a great surprise when, months later, Fred was arrested and his illicit crop seized. Fred could not figure out what had caused his scheme to unravel. Can you?

CLUES: 48 / ANSWER: 89

THE SKY DIVER

Pierre went skydiving near his home in Dallas, Texas. As a result, Pierre saved his brother's life. Strangely though, his brother lived in Boston and hadn't seen or spoken to his brother Pierre for a great many years. How could this miracle have taken place?

CLUES: 48–49 / ANSWER: 92

EYES ON THE PRIZE

The Stardust Lounge was holding its annual raffle. First prize was $1,000 dollars in cash. Hopeful participants wrote their names on slips of paper which were then placed in a large bowl. When Alexander Turnbull's name was announced as the winner, he was both surprised and excited, yet he did not claim the money. Why not?

CLUES: 49 / ANSWER: 82

THE ALASKAN DREAM

Scott is an expert outdoorsman, pursuing his dream by living alone in the remote Alaskan wilderness. Scott has everything he needs, and would prefer to remain a recluse, yet he will have to leave his home in four years. Why?

CLUES: 50 / ANSWER: 77

A BRIDGE TO FEAR

On her way to work one blustery winter day, Patty slipped and fell over the railing of the world's highest suspension bridge. She was wearing only her regular office attire, yet she was not harmed in any way. How could that be?

CLUES: 50 / ANSWER: 78

PETTY CASH

When Pauline's house was burglarized, five dollars were taken from a dresser drawer. Nothing else was stolen or damaged. After filing a claim with her insurance company, Pauline was paid one thousand dollars for her loss. What was the reason behind this settlement?

CLUES: 50 / ANSWER: 88

FEAST OR FAMINE

After months of subsisting on a starvation diet, Paul finally obtained some decent food. Why, then, did he pass up this opportunity to enjoy a perfectly good meal?

CLUES: 51 / ANSWER: 82

An Axe to Grind

When Jerry, a lumberjack known for exaggeration, boasted of cutting down a one-hundred-year-old maple tree in ten seconds using only a small axe, his friend Mac had had enough. He challenged Jerry to prove his incredible claim. How did the brawny braggart succeed?

CLUES: 51 / ANSWER: 77

The Root of the Problem

Mr. Finkel was an avid gardener who was very proud of his landscaping and horticultural skills. Unfortunately, Mr. Finkel's hobby caused the death of a neighbor after he planted a tree in his backyard. How could his gentle pastime have turned deadly?

CLUES: 51 / ANSWER: 90

THE SKY'S THE LIMIT

Henry, a poor but lucky fisherman, finds a treasure map that promises great wealth–beyond his wildest dreams. He ultimately retrieves the loot which lay buried on an island barely a day's sail from his home. Why did Henry wait three months to retrieve the loot?

CLUES: 52 / ANSWER: 92

THE DISCOURAGING DISCOVERY

During the aftermath of a violent storm, Vern is pleased to find that his house has come through unscathed. Later that day, Vern discovers that he has suffered a large loss in the value of his property. What led Vern to this unfortunate conclusion?

CLUES: 52–53 / ANSWER: 80

THE EXPERT PILOT

A man is flying a plane. When the engine begins to stall, the pilot immediately switches to his reserve fuel tank. Later in the flight, the landing gear warning light comes on, yet the pilot is not concerned with this new, potentially lethal problem. Why not?

CLUES: 53 / ANSWER: 81

WHAT'S IT ALL ABOUT?

Mack goes on an eating binge for several days, which ends up costing him two million dollars. How?

CLUES: 53 / ANSWER: 93

THE MYSTERIOUS MOTORIST

Every so often, Jennifer pulls off to the side of the road and opens the trunk of her car. She doesn't get anything out of the trunk or put anything into it. Can you give a reason for this seemingly strange activity?

CLUES: 54 / ANSWER: 87

A SENSE OF DIRECTION

On the first day of a business trip to Japan, B.J. arrives at a large office building. She had never been there before, and could not read any of the signs. Without seeing or talking with anyone, she quickly makes her way through a labyrinth of hallways to arrive at her destination. How?

CLUES: 54 / ANSWER: 90

MOVING DAY

Herb gets a job in a new city. On the day of his move, Herb causes a traffic jam without ever leaving his home. How does Herb create such a monumental disturbance?

CLUES: 54 / ANSWER: 87

I BID THEE FAREWELL

Dee places an ad soliciting bids for the construction of a new office building. In response, she receives two bids. Without opening either, she immediately throws one away. Why did she make such a rash decision?

CLUES: 55 / ANSWER: 84

SHED SOME LIGHT

A hermit inherits a large amount of money and has a new house built. Although he enjoys his new home immensely, he only uses the lights during the day. Why does he do this?

CLUES: 55 / ANSWER: 91

A HUNTING ACCIDENT

Mick often went hunting in the extensive marshlands which surrounded the local airport. One day, a plane was forced to make a crash landing. Although Mick never fired his rifle, or any other weapon, his hunting trip was directly responsible for the tragedy. How did Mick's hunting trip turn deadly?

CLUES: 55 / ANSWER: 84

Down on the Farm

Two farmers, Jedro and Jason, have farms that are adjacent to each other. They both plant the same crop and use identical techniques. Furthermore, both of the farms measure ten miles long by ten miles wide. Why, then, is Jedro able to produce ten percent more grain than Jason every year?

Clues: 56 / Answer: 81

Long Time No See

Kathy receives a call from an old friend and roommate on the phone. She has known this person intimately for years, yet Kathy does not recognize her friend's voice. How can this be?

Clues: 56 / Answer: 86.

Whose Vault Is It?

A burglar is stealing two bars of gold, each so heavy he cannot lift them above his waist. On his way out of the vault, he suddenly sees a security camera ahead. Thinking quickly, he disguises himself without putting down the gold bars. How?

Clues: 56 / Answer: 94

On the Boardwalk

Patrick has a regular delivery route along the Myrtle Beach boardwalk. Each day he makes his deliveries using a handcart and returns to his shop at the north end of the boardwalk. Although he is not physically tired, Patrick always finds that the return trip, with his now empty cart, is more difficult. Why?

CLUES: 57 / ANSWER: 88

THE SECRET MEETING

A man and a woman meet at their regular time and place. They have an intimate conversation together, yet neither one can describe the other to their friends. Why?

CLUES: 57–58 / ANSWER: 90

TEMPORARY HOUSING

Jake builds a house, and although anyone would be satisfied with the construction, he knows he'll have to rebuild it in fifteen years. Why?

CLUES: 58 / ANSWER: 92

A Customs Conundrum

Eric spends his vacation in the Swiss Alps. Unfortunately, he ends up spending the greater part of his visit in the hospital, after having taken a nasty spill while skiing. On his return trip home to the U.S., the authorities do not ask him to show his passport. Why not?

CLUES: 58 / ANSWER: 79

The Yard Sale

After buying a new oven, Gerald sold his old one to a stranger. Although the stranger offered to pay cash, Gerald, nonetheless, had a very good reason for insisting that the transaction take place at a bank. Rather than be offended, the stranger clearly understood the reason for this unusual request. Why did Gerald make this demand?

CLUES: 58–59 / ANSWER: 94

The Master Mechanic

Gary, a highly skilled auto mechanic, climbed under the chassis of Shawn's midnight-blue Pontiac GTO. Ten minutes later he climbed out from under the car. Gary did not inspect or repair the automobile, nor did he offer any professional advice to the car's owner. In fact, Shawn knew full well that Gary had never even touched the vehicle. Immediately afterwards, and as a result of what had just occurred, Shawn unhesitatingly paid Gary five hundred dollars. Why would he do this?

CLUES: 59 / ANSWER: 86

THE KING'S TEST

An eccentric king wanted to find the smartest person in his kingdom. He had one bucket of milk and another bucket of water, both filled to the rim. He then said, "Whoever can mix these together to form a 50/50 mixture without using anything other than these two buckets will receive a thousand gold coins." How did one man finally succeed?

CLUES: 59 / ANSWER: 84–85

HARD OF DARKNESS

Tim and Ralph were the best of friends. They were also very competitive. Over the years, Tim and Ralph have met each and every challenge, both mental and physical, posed by the other. One day, Tim succeeds in posing a challenge that Ralph cannot possibly meet. What is the challenge?

CLUES: 59–60 / ANSWER: 83

CRUSTACEAN VACATION

After being away on business for a week, Milton checked with his son to see how their crabbing business had prospered during his absence. When his son reported that things had slacked off all week, the father was disappointed, yet he trusted his son's response. The next day, as they prepared to launch their boat, Milton began scolding his son for lying. How did he know his son had deceived him?

CLUES: 60 / ANSWER: 79

ATTORNEY CLIENT PRIVILEGE

Sam is talking to his lawyer in jail. They are very upset because the judge has refused to grant bail. Oddly enough, at the end of the conversation Sam is allowed to leave the jail. Why?

CLUES: 61 / ANSWER: 77

HARRY THE HOMEOWNER

Harry goes out and buys a new house. One day he returns home to find that all of the furniture in the house has been completely rearranged. Strangely, Harry is not in the least bit surprised or irritated, even though he didn't ask anyone to do this. Why?

CLUES: 61 / ANSWER: 83

THE BIG GAME

One of the most prominent citizens of Chicago once offered highly prized football tickets to forty people whom he despised. Can you explain his unusual generosity?

CLUES: 61 / ANSWER: 78

FIRST EDITION

Mr. Jones drives a hundred miles to the nearest book store. He pays twenty dollars of his hard-earned money to purchase a first edition of a new book. After many hours of reading, he concludes that the book is poorly written, boring, and inaccurate. Rather than be upset, Mr. Jones is instead greatly pleased with his purchase. Why would this be?

CLUES: 62 / ANSWER: 83

A REVERTING DEVELOPMENT

An artist, working in his private studio, had just finished a new creation, so he decided to take a break and visit an old friend. During his visit a violent storm erupted. The artist soon realized that his work of art would be ruined. How did he know?

CLUES: 62 / ANSWER: 90

MONUMENTAL ACHIEVEMENT

A man makes his way to the top of a hundred-foot-high

monument in the center of a small town. He then jumps off the monument without the aide of a parachute, glider, or other such device. He is not harmed in any way. How did he manage to do this?

CLUES: 62 / ANSWER: 87

ROOM DESPAIR

A man paid thousands of dollars to build an addition onto his primary residence. Yet, after the construction was completed, he never went into that part of the house again. Why?

CLUES: 63 / ANSWER: 90

THE PILOT'S PUZZLE

A pilot was in an emergency situation, and needed to land his aircraft in unfamiliar territory. He immediately spotted two possible landing sites, the first of which was a flat and open field. The second site was inhabited by grazing livestock and had a rough terrain. Why, then, did he choose the latter?

CLUES: 63–64 / ANSWER: 89

AN EXPLOSIVE SITUATION

While at work one day, a man hears a loud explosion and is thrown hundreds of feet through the air. This is witnessed by many people, but no one attempts to give him aid. Why didn't they help the man?

CLUES: 64 / ANSWER: 81

LEAVE IT OR NOT

Elizabeth lives in a neighborhood known for its well-tended and manicured lawns. Yet, for some reason, while Elizabeth is busily raking up leaves from her trees, all of her neighbors are content to simply ignore theirs. Can you explain this situation?

CLUES: 64 / ANSWER: 85

SHORE SIGHTED

A group of friends set out for a leisurely day of boating and become stranded when the motor dies. The boat has no other means of reaching shore, and isn't equipped with a radio, but the friends do find some flares. Still, although they are within sight of hundreds of people on shore, they are not rescued for several hours. Why does rescue take so long?

CLUES: 65 / ANSWER: 91

The Perfect Crime

Rocky bludgeons an acquaintance to death. He makes no attempt to hide the evidence, and the next day he returns to the scene of the crime along with some mutual friends of the victim. As they arrive at the victim's home, Rocky sees that the police have already discovered the body. Although it could have placed Rocky at great risk of criminal prosecution, he freely admits to having been alone with the victim on the previous day. Why?

CLUES: 65 / ANSWER: 88

Express Checkout

Barry notices a boy and his father in a grocery store, neither of whom he has ever seen before. Although he doesn't speak to anyone and there is nothing unusual going on at the time, he calls the police moments later. What compels him to make this call?

CLUES: 65 / ANSWER: 81–82

The Debating Club

Four longtime friends share a passion for debating. They have met every other Saturday night for the past ten years. There are periodic interruptions in their conversations that last a few minutes. This happens regularly, yet no one thinks twice about it and their debates always continue to a satisfactory conclusion. Can you explain these odd interruptions?

CLUES: 66 / ANSWER: 80

BILL'S BIRTHDAY SURPRISE

Marion's husband, Bill, was a slob who avoided bathing at all cost. On his wife's birthday, Bill decided to surprise her by taking a bath without having to be asked. Instead of being pleased, Marion was upset. Why?

CLUES: 66 / ANSWER: 78

THE PHONED-IN MESSAGE

Kathleen used the courtesy phone in the lobby of the hotel to call the hotel's front desk and leave a message for her husband. It would have been easier for her to walk to the front desk and leave the message in person. Why did she choose to use the phone?

CLUES: 66 / ANSWER: 88

MAKING THE GRADE

Alphonso was taking an important exam. Although the examiner was standing twenty feet away and had his back turned, he interrupted Alphonso by saying, "You can stop right now, I know you are cheating." What led to Alphonso's undoing?

CLUES: 67 / ANSWER: 86

SOMETHING'S UP

A man suspected his wife of having an affair. He confronted her, but she claimed to have spent the entire day at home by herself. She had taken care that no items were left behind by her lover, but her husband soon found the only clue he needed to prove to himself that his suspicions were justified. What did he find?

CLUES: 67 / ANSWER: 92

MOURNING GLORIA

Gloria attended the funeral of a total stranger. She did not play any part in the funeral. In fact, the funeral would have taken place in exactly the same manner without her presence. Why did she attend?

CLUES: 68 / ANSWER: 87

THE CINEMA SNEAK

After three attempts, Larry was finally able to sneak in the back door of a movie theater, and began watching the movie which had just started. After a few minutes, he left. Later in the week, he paid to see the same movie. Why?

CLUES: 68 / ANSWER: 79

BAD MEDICINE

Mel had consultations with Dr. Greenwood over several days in an attempt to cure his condition. When Mel was finally cured, he immediately strangled the doctor to death. Why?

CLUES: 68 / ANSWER: 77–78

THE LETTER

Danielle is eagerly awaiting the arrival of a very important letter. The letter contains vital information that could possibly save her life. Yet when it arrives, Danielle does not read the letter and in fact never even opens it. Why?

CLUES: 69 / ANSWER: 85

THE POEM

After reading a lengthy poem, a man realized that it had been originally written in another language. Although he had no prior knowledge of the poem or the poet, how did he come to this conclusion?

CLUES: 69 / ANSWER: 89

FINDERS KEEPERS

One day, Ted finds a solid gold letter opener along the side of a busy highway. Although he is poor and would gladly pawn it for money, Ted knows that he will not be able to do so. Why?

CLUES: 69 / ANSWER: 82

Jury Duty

In most states, a jury must vote unanimously in order to render a verdict of guilty. In this particular case, when the final vote was taken, one of the people in the room did not vote. However, the defendant was found guilty. How is this possible?

CLUES: 70 / ANSWER: 84

Peculiar Parking

Sam is a truck driver for Consolidated Freight Lines. His route takes him from Baltimore to Cleveland; Cleveland to St. Louis; then back home to Baltimore. When Sam is in Cleveland he always takes up two extra parking spaces before going to sleep in his truck. In St. Louis, however, he only uses one space. Why would he do this?

CLUES: 70–71 / ANSWER: 88

A Golden Opportunity

Bill challenged his friend to retrieve a heavy gold coin from the center of a bucket which had been half filled with dried peas. He then set forth the following rules:

1. No peas could be touched or removed.
2. The bucket could not be damaged in any way.
3. Nothing could be placed in the bucket other than one's hand.

How did his friend meet the challenge?

CLUES: 71 / ANSWER: 83

Diamonds Are Forever

An eccentric billionaire bought a two-million-dollar diamond. He took it to the world's foremost safe maker and had him seal the diamond inside a seamless steel box. He then announced: "Whoever can remove the diamond from the box without taking the box from this room or using any tools whatsoever can keep the gem." After years of attempts, how did one man succeed in this quest?

Clues: 71 / Answer: 80

The Singing Kidnapper

Kidnapper Karl would always sing his demands to the police. Why did he communicate in this strange way?

Clues: 72 / Answer: 91

Dead Connection

One night, two men committed suicide within minutes of each other. They had never met, nor did they even know of the other's existence. Yet, if the first man had not taken his own life, the other might still be alive as well. Why should this be so?

CLUES: 72 / ANSWER: 79

Language Skills

For most Americans, the inability to read and write in their native language would preclude them from working for the U.S. Government. Yet, at one point in our history, certain individuals with this trait were highly sought after. Who were these individuals and why did Uncle Sam want them?

CLUES: 73 / ANSWER: 85

It's About Time

Reginald took great pains to locate and to go to a renowned clock maker where he purchased a clock which was purported to remain accurate to within one second per month. Reginald gently transported the clock to his study and mounted it securely on the wall. Later, Reginald brought the clock back to the shop and complained that it had lost over three minutes in less than a month. On hearing the story, the clock maker replied, "But you never told me where your study was located!" Why would that matter?

CLUES: 73 / ANSWER: 84

Fast Food

Mike lives in a sparsely populated rural area. His commute to work takes an average of 70 minutes each day. Likewise, at the end of his shift, Mike spends an average of 70 minutes returning home. Considering the fact that Mike's lunch break is only 30 minutes long, how does he manage to spend it in the comfort of his own home?

CLUES: 73 / ANSWER: 82

The Love Note

Every morning, Victoria would wake up to find a love note left behind by her thoughtful husband, Mark. One morning, after looking and failing to see the expected note, Victoria despondently began to prepare for work. A few minutes later, Victoria was pleased to find Mark's amorous message in plain view and in a very conspicuous location. Why hadn't Victoria noticed it earlier?

CLUES: 74 / ANSWER: 86

Sticky Fingers

Joan felt comforted by how routine her life had become. Even her packed lunch never varied from day to day. Imagine her dismay, when someone began stealing her meal from the lunchroom refrigerator. To make matters worst, the thief would taunt her by placing the empty bag back in the refrigerator. Joan finally devised a plan to reveal the culprit, without changing the contents of her lunch. How did she finally nab the thief?

CLUES: 74 / ANSWER: 92

THE EVIDENCE

Little did Ken know, that by merely walking into the room, he had just enabled a notorious mobster to be set free. How could this simple act have led to the release of a clearly guilty criminal?

CLUES: 74–75 / ANSWER: 81

CREATURE DISCOMFORT

While traveling down a dark and lonely road, Bart heard a rustling noise coming from the woods. In an attempt to frighten away whatever creature lurked close by, Bart threw a rock in the general direction of the noise. The rock scored a direct hit. Although Bart succeeded in scaring away the animal, he regretted his choice of actions. Why?

CLUES: 75 / ANSWER: 79

AN ALARMING CHANGE OF PACE

William makes his living by cutting in front of people while they are standing in line and by setting off alarms. He does not work alone, yet he rarely talks to any of his colleagues. How does William earn a living?

CLUES: 76 / ANSWER: 77

CLUES

A Fire Escape

Q: Was Nicole physically capable of walking on her own?
A: Yes

Q: Was the fire blocking Nicole's path of escape?
A: No

Q: Was Nicole sleeping in her own home?
A: No

Q: Could Nicole have left the building if the fire had not occurred?
A: No

The Unsuccessful Suicide

Q: Was the man really trying to commit suicide?
A: Yes

Q: If he had jumped from the building the day before, would he have been arrested?
A: Yes

Q: Did the police think the man was trying to commit suicide?
A: No

Q: Were the police at the scene solely for the purpose of saving his life?
A: No

Q: Was the pub known for having a shady reputation?
A: Yes

Q: Did J.P. want the thief to steal the money?
A: Yes

Q: Was J.P. a criminal himself?
A: Yes

Q: Did J.P. learn something from watching the thief spend the money?
A: Yes

TO TELL A MOCKINGBIRD

Q: Did Christopher have something to gain by only turning in John?
A: No

Q: If John had been a total stranger, would Christopher have turned him in?

A: No

Q: Did Christopher learn of Bob's illegal activities in a different setting than he did John's?

A: Yes

MORE THAN HE BARGAINED FOR

Q: Is there something that Bert sees which causes this realization?

A: Yes

Q: Was Bert's retirement nest egg stored in a safe place?

A: No

Q: If Bert was window shopping in the same store a minute earlier or later, would he have come to the same conclusion?

A: No

THE FRUSTRATED FUTURES TRADER

Q: Is the location of Joe's home important?
A: Yes

Q: Does Joe's frustration occur at a specific place and/or time each day?
A: Yes

Q: Is there something unusual about Joe's car?
A: Yes

AN UNTIMELY DEATH

Q: Is it important to know what type of animal Roscoe was?
A: Yes

Q: Would it help to determine Cal's occupation?
A: Yes

Q: Did Cal and his co-workers fear that they might die from the same cause as Roscoe?
A: Yes

THE LONG ROAD AHEAD

Q: Could Bubba have taken a shortcut to reach his destination?
A: No

Q: Could Bubba have driven 399 miles and walked the remaining mile to reach his goal?
A: No

Q: Did other people undertake the same journey at the same time?
A: Yes

The Prison Break

Q: Was Jim ever convicted of a crime?
A: No

Q: Was Jim ever accused of committing a crime?
A: No

Q: Did Jim know that he wouldn't be taken back into custody?
A: Yes

Wood That I Could

Q: Did Tom light the fire to keep warm?
A: No

Q: Would Tom have lit the fire if it wasn't raining?
A: Yes

Q: Does the rain have any significance as to why Tom lit the fire?
A: No

Q: Does Tom have only a limited amount of firewood?
A: Yes

A Shooting at Midnight

Q: Was the man trying to hit something?
A: Yes

Q: Was the man injured in any way?
A: No

Q: Did the man want to see the sunrise?
A: No

Q: Was the intended target important?
A: Yes

EXECUTION AT DAWN

Q: Were all seven marksmen aiming at the same man?
A: Yes

Q: Were all seven rifles in good working order?
A: Yes

Q: After examining the body, were they surprised to find only six bullets in the man's body?
A: No

THE LEAKY BOAT

Q: Did Al attempt to keep the boat from sinking?
A: No

Q: Was this an unusual occurrence?
A: No

Q: Did Al have a reason for leaving the boat underwater?
A: Yes

Q: Was the sinking beneficial to the boat in some way?
A: Yes

WONDER WOMAN

Q: Is there anything physically unusual about the woman that permits her to perform this feat?
A: No

Q: Are there any special conditions that allowed her to accomplish this task?
A: Yes

Q: Is the woman's occupation important?
A: Yes

By the Time I Get to Phoenix

Q: Did Nick plan to make this drive in another country?

A: No

Q: Could Nick have actually performed this feat if Frank had asked him to?

A: Yes

Q: Could the average person have accomplished this task?

A: Yes

Dead Men Tell No Tales

Q: Was anyone in the search party aware of who the criminal was before arriving at the crime scene?

A: No

Q: Did the murderer turn himself in?

A: No

Q: Was the time of death important to the solving of the crime?

A: Yes

Out of Bounds

Q: Did the fans realize what the problem was?

A: Yes

Q: Did they have all of the equipment necessary to play the game after the field goal was kicked?

A: No

Q: Does it matter where the game was being played?

A: Yes

SWIMMING WITH THE FISHES

Q: Did something prevent him from reaching shore?
A: Yes

Q: Did the man fall into the lake from a boat?
A: No

Q: Does it matter what type of fishing he was doing?
A: Yes

THE DOMINO EFFECT

Q: Did Charlotte use any tools or aids to help her do this?
A: No

Q: Was the sugar held within a container?
A: No

Q: Was the sugar in powder form?
A: No

THE RUNAWAY

Q: Was Alex afraid to chase the man?
A: No

Q: Is the item that the man took significant?
A: Yes

Q: Did Alex know the man who took the object away from him?
A: Yes

SHORTCHANGED

Q: Was her bookie's phone busy?
A: No

Q: Did anyone stop Minnie from making the phone call?
A: No

Q: Did Minnie ever make a phone call?
A: No

MONEY TROUBLES

Q: Would the man have feared for his life if he had left the jail?

A: No

Q: If his bail had been posted by someone else, would he leave?

A: Yes

Q: Does the type of crime he was charged with have any relevance?

A: Yes

Q: Was the man guilty of the crime with which he had been charged?

A: Yes

PHOTO FINISHED

Q: Did the videotape tip the police off?
A: Yes

Q: Were the tapes filmed in the South Pacific?
A: Yes

Q: If Ben had filmed only during the day, would he have been caught?
A: No

KEEP ON TRUCKIN'

Q: Did Lewis see something that led him to this conclusion?

A: Yes

Q: Is there something about their physical appearance that gave Lewis a clue to their origin?

A: Yes

Q: Is it important that they drive on the left-hand side of the road in Australia?

A: Yes

MR. GRAY'S ANATOMY

Q: Did Mr. Gray simply want to commit suicide?

A: No

Q: Would it have been legal for Mr. Gray's parents to comply with his request?

A: Yes

Q: Might Mr. Gray have made the same request if it had been 1892 instead of 1992?

A: No

POTTED PLANTS

Q: Was Fred detected through a type of surveillance?

A: No

Q: Did Fred's day-to-day activities appear suspicious?

A: No

Q: Was there something Fred needed to obtain which caused him to come under suspicion?

A: Yes

Q: Could Fred have purchased this at a regular store?

A: No

THE SKY DIVER

Q: Did Pierre discover something which was a help to his brother?

A: No

Q: If Pierre had stayed home that day, could he have saved his brother's life?
A: No

Q: Did Pierre communicate some information to his brother which saved his brother's life?
A: No

EYES ON THE PRIZE

Q: Was Alexander afraid to claim the prize?
A: No

Q: Did he fill out an entry form?
A: No

Q: Did someone else fill his name in on the form?
A: Yes

The Alaskan Dream

Q: Was something going to happen that would destroy Scott's home?

A: No

Q: Did Scott need to return to civilization in order to buy food or clothing?

A: No

Q: Would Scott have been in danger if he ignored the four-year deadline?

A: Yes

A Bridge to Fear

Q: Is the type of work Patty did relevant?

A: No

Q: Did something cushion the impact of Patty's fall from the bridge?

A: No

Q: Could the average person have survived this fall?

A: Yes

Q: Does it matter where Patty was located on the bridge when she fell?

A: Yes

Petty Cash

Q: Did Pauline falsify the claim she made to her insurance company?

A: No

Q: Was there anything unusual about the stolen money?

A: Yes

Feast or Famine

Q: Was Paul allergic to the food?
A: No

Q: Was Paul on a hunger strike before he received the food?
A: No

Q: Does it matter that he was already malnourished to begin with?
A: Yes

An Axe to Grind

Q: Was the tree healthy at the time Jerry cut it down?
A: Yes

Q: Was there something special about Jerry?
A: No

Q: Would this tree supply a lot of firewood?
A: No

The Root of the Problem

Q: Did the tree obstruct or hinder anyone's view?
A: No

Q: If Mr. Finkel had planted the same tree in a different spot in his yard, would the outcome have been the same?
A: No

Q: If Mr. Finkel had planted the tree a day later or a day earlier, would he have been responsible for his neighbor's death?
A: No

Q: Was Henry able to travel when he first found the map?

A: Yes

Q: If someone else had discovered the map, would they also have waited?

A: Yes

Q: Was there something unusual about the map?

A: Yes

The Discouraging Discovery

Q: Did Vern discover that his house was not worth as much as he had thought?

A: Yes

Q: Did the storm uncover or disturb something that led Vern to discover the loss?
A: Yes

Q: Was storm damage elsewhere on the property the cause of the loss of value?
A: No

Q: Is the age of Vern's house significant?
A: Yes

THE EXPERT PILOT

Q: Is the plane capable of landing without using landing gear?
A: No

Q: Does he plan to parachute out of the plane?
A: No

Q: Is the man a military pilot?
A: Yes

Q: Did this occur during wartime?
A: Yes

WHAT'S IT ALL ABOUT?

Q: Did Mack spend all or a good part of this money while on his eating binge?
A: No

Q: If Mack had started his binge one month later, would it still have cost him the money?
A: No

Q: Is it important that Mack had gained a lot of weight.
A: Yes

The Mysterious Motorist

Q: Was Jennifer having car trouble?
A: No

Q: Does Jennifer do this on a regular basis?
A: Yes

Q: Could any of the passing motorists tell why Jennifer had opened the trunk?
A: Yes

Q: Was she working when this occurred?
A: Yes

A Sense of Direction

Q: Were there any other visual clues which helped B.J. to find her destination?
A: No

Q: Did B.J. hear something that helped her find her way?
A: No

Q: Could B.J. have done this in any other building?
A: No

Moving Day

Q: If Herb had moved on another day, would he still have caused a traffic jam?
A: Yes

Q: Did Herb have to pack anything prior to moving?
A: No

Q: Did Herb live in a traditional type of home?
A: No

I Bid Thee Farewell

Q: Did Dee know beforehand that the bid would be un-
acceptable?
A: No

Q: If the bid had been received via fax machine, would
it have been considered?
A: Yes

Q: Is the type of business that Dee works for important?
A: Yes

Shed Some Light

Q: Is he saving money?
A: No

Q: Is he trying to hide for some reason?
A: No

Q: Does he have electricity available at all times?
A: No

A Hunting Accident

Q: Is this a regular-size plane, not a model or toy?
A: Yes

Q: Does Mick use an unusual hunting method?
A: Yes

Q: Did he cause something to collide with the plane?
A: Yes

Q: If the plane had been propeller driven, would it
have crashed?
A: No

DOWN ON THE FARM

Q: Did both farmers have access to the same water supply?
A: Yes

Q: Could a passerby determine why Jedro's farm produces more grain each year?
A: Yes

Q: Had the two farmers exchanged properties, would Jedro continue to produce more grain than Jason?
A: No

LONG TIME NO SEE

Q: Did something happen to her friend's voice?
A: No

Q: Did Kathy have any physical or mental disabilities, such as deafness or amnesia?
A: No

Q: Had they ever spoken to each other before?
A: No

WHOSE VAULT IS IT?

Q: Was he wearing anything on his head?
A: No

Q: Did the criminal cover his face with something?
A: Yes

Q: Did he cover his face with something burglars typically use while robbing banks?
A: No

Q: Is the boardwalk completely flat?
A: Yes

Q: Is Patrick carrying anything back with him on his return trip?
A: No

Q: Is the type of merchandise important?
A: Yes

Q: Does the merchandise assist him in moving the cart?
A: Yes

THE SECRET MEETING

Q: Is the man's profession relevant?
A: Yes

Q: Does the man speak intimately with other people on a regular basis?
A: Yes

Q: Is the exact location of their meetings important?
A: Yes

TEMPORARY HOUSING

Q: Did Jake use materials that would last only 15 years?
A: No

Q: Did Jake build a traditional house?
A: No

A CUSTOMS CONUNDRUM

Q: Was Eric hiding from the Customs authorities?
A: No

Q: Was Eric an important official who was exempt from this procedure?
A: No

Q: Did the type of transportation Eric was using matter?
A: No

Q: Did the customs officials check the passports of any of the passengers?
A: Yes

THE YARD SALE

Q: Did Gerald know how to count?
A: Yes

Q: Did the man have the correct currency?
A: Yes

Q: Would he have insisted on going to the bank, had he sold the oven to a friend?
A: No

THE MASTER MECHANIC

Q: Did Shawn expect Gary to do any work on the car?
A: No

Q: Is Gary's occupation important?
A: No

Q: Would it help to know where Shawn's car was parked at the time Gary climbed under it?
A: Yes

THE KING'S TEST

Q: Does the man pour the milk or water at any time?
A: No

Q: Does the man accomplish this task quickly?
A: No

Q: Could milk and vodka, for example, be used for the test?
A: No

HARD OF DARKNESS

Q: Are Tim and Ralph of the same sex?
A: Yes

Q: Did the challenge require some specific knowledge that Ralph could not possibly have possessed?
A: No

Q: Could the average man win the bet?
A: Yes

Q: If you looked at the two friends, would you know why Ralph was unable to meet the challenge?

A: Yes

Crustacean Vacation

Q: Did Milton check with someone else to see if his son was lying?

A: No

Q: Would it help to know where the crab boat had been stored?

A: Yes

Q: Did Milton have reason to believe the boat had not been used during his absence?

A: Yes

ATTORNEY CLIENT PRIVILEGE

Q: Is it important why Sam was in jail?
A: Yes

Q: Did Sam's lawyer provide Sam with any legal assistance that day?
A: No

Q: Could Sam have been able to get out of jail if his lawyer had *not* been there?
A: Yes

HARRY THE HOMEOWNER

Q: Does it matter why Harry bought the house?
A: Yes

Q: Did Harry know who had moved the furniture?
A: Yes

Q: Could anyone have lived in this house?
A: No

THE BIG GAME

Q: Was the man trying to get rid of tickets?
A: No

Q: Was the game upcoming and scheduled for a convenient time and place?
A: Yes

Q: Did the people who were offered the tickets actually get to use them to go to the game?
A: No

Q: Did the man have the tickets available to give away?
A: No

First Edition

Q: If Mr. Jones had found it accurate and interesting, would he be upset?

A: Yes

Q: Does Mr. Jones have special knowledge of the book's subject matter?

A: Yes

Q: Does Mr. Jones have a financial interest in the book's success or failure?

A: Yes

A Reverting Development

Q: If he had been at home, could he have prevented the work of art from being ruined?

A: No

Q: Is it important to know what type of artist he was?

A: Yes

Q: Does it matter what material the artist was using?

A: Yes

Monumental Achievement

Q: Was there something special about the man which enabled him to perform this feat?

A: No

Q: Did the man fear being injured as he leaped off the monument?

A: No

Q: Did something slow his descent as he traveled down the side of the monument?

A: Yes

Q: Was he avoiding going into the addition for some reason?
A: No

Q: Did he have a specific reason for not entering the addition?
A: Yes

Q: Was there something unusual about his house?
A: No

THE PILOT'S PUZZLE

Q: If the pilot had landed on the other field, could it have been life-threatening?
A: Yes

Q: Was the presence of the livestock in the field a deciding factor?
A: Yes

Q: Was the man a military pilot?
A: Yes

Q: Was the man flying during wartime?
A: Yes

AN EXPLOSIVE SITUATION

Q: Did the man die in the explosion?
A: No

Q: Were the people who saw what had happened startled by it?
A: No

Q: Was the man prepared for this explosion?
A: Yes

Q: Had this ever happened to the man before?
A: Yes

LEAVE IT OR NOT

Q: Is Elizabeth at all concerned about the inaction of her neighbors with regard to their leaves?
A: No

Q: Is the time of year important?
A: Yes

Q: Could Elizabeth have prevented the need to rake up the leaves?
A: Yes

SHORE SIGHTED

Q: Did the stranded people fire any of the flares to indicate that they needed help?
A: Yes

Q: Were the people on shore able to see the flares?
A: Yes

Q: Did the people on shore think that the flares were being used for some other reason?
A: Yes

THE PERFECT CRIME

Q: Did Rocky take any steps to hide his crime?
A: No

Q: Is there a way Rocky could have planned this perfect crime?
A: No

Q: Did Rocky actually want to avoid being implicated in the crime?
A: Yes

EXPRESS CHECKOUT

Q: Is it likely this string of events would have taken place in a department store?
A: No

Q: Could this have taken place thirty years ago?
A: No

Q: Does what merchandise Barry was purchasing matter?
A: Yes

THE DEBATING CLUB

Q: Are these interruptions a common occurance at most debating clubs?

A: No

Q: Are the interruptions caused by something or someone unrelated to the group?

A: No

Q: Could these interruptions have been avoided by the group?

A: No

BILL'S BIRTHDAY SURPRISE

Q: Would Marion have asked Bill to bathe that day?

A: No

Q: Would Marion have been upset if Bill had taken a bath the day before?

A: No

Q: Did Bill fill the tub himself?

A: No

Q: Did anything else unusual happen that day?

A: Yes

THE PHONED-IN MESSAGE

Q: Did Kathleen have some difficulty in communicating with people directly?

A: No

Q: Was the content of the message relevant?

A: No

Q: Is her calling from the lobby phone important?

A: Yes

MAKING THE GRADE

Q: Did the examiner watch Alphonso in a mirror?
A: No

Q: Did this exam test Alphonso's knowledge of a certain subject matter?
A: No

Q: Was Alphonso taking an oral exam?
A: Yes

Q: Was Alphonso taking a medical exam?
A: Yes

SOMETHING'S UP

Q: Was anything missing from the house?
A: No

Q: Was anything brought into the house?
A: No

Q: Was anything moved within the house?
A: Yes

MOURNING GLORIA

Q: Was Gloria attending the funeral on behalf of someone else?
A: No

Q: Is the circumstance of the man's death important?
A: Yes

Q: Was Gloria trying to profit from the man's death?
A: Yes

THE CINEMA SNEAK

Q: Was Larry afraid of being caught and punished for sneaking into the movie?
A: No

Q: Was Larry unable to fully enjoy the movie for some reason?
A: Yes

Q: Would Larry have reacted the same way regardless of what movie was playing?
A: No

BAD MEDICINE

Q: Would Mel have killed the doctor before he was cured?
A: No

Q: Does it matter what kind of doctor Mel went to?
A: Yes

Q: Is Mel's medical condition important?
A: Yes

THE LETTER

Q: Could Danielle have read the letter if she had just opened it?

A: Yes

Q: Did Danielle know who had sent the letter?

A: Yes

Q: If the letter had been opened, would it have lost its value?

A: Yes

THE POEM

Q: Did the meaning of any of the words in the poem lead the man to his conclusion?

A: No

Q: Did the subject of the poem matter?

A: No

Q: Would the man have come to that realization, if the writing had been prose?

A: No

FINDERS KEEPERS

Q: Did Ted know who the letter opener belonged to?

A: No

Q: If Ted had found anything else, would he have been able to sell it?

A: No

Q: Did Ted know that someone else would take the letter opener away from him?

A: Yes

JURY DUTY

Q: Were all of the jury members present at the time of the vote?

A: Yes

Q: Were there any alternate jurors present in the jury room?

A: No

Q: Was there anything uncommon about any of the jury members?

A: Yes

PECULIAR PARKING

Q: Is there a shortage of parking spaces at any of the three terminals?

A: No

Q: Is parking in extra spaces a common occurrence with other truck drivers driving the same route?

A: No

Q: If Sam had stayed in a hotel, would he have parked the truck using extra spaces?
A: No

Q: Is Sam's ethnic background important?
A: Yes

A GOLDEN OPPORTUNITY

Q: If the bucket had been filled to the rim with dried peas, would Bill's friend have been able to get the coin?
A: No

Q: Did Bill's friend use tools or equipment to remove the coin?
A: Yes

Q: Is the exact location of the coin important?
A: Yes

Q: Had the coin been placed slightly off center, would Bill's friend have been able to retrieve it?
A: No

DIAMONDS ARE FOREVER

Q: Armed with the proper knowledge, could anyone have removed the diamond from the box?
A: Yes

Q: Could the man have removed the diamond if he had only been allowed to handle the box for a short period of time?
A: No

Q: Could the man have removed a two-million-dollar pearl from the same box?
A: No

THE SINGING KIDNAPPER

Q: Was Karl trying to disguise his voice?
A: No

Q: Was it important that Karl phoned in his demands?
A: Yes

Q: Was Karl doing what he could to keep his messages brief?
A: Yes

DEAD CONNECTION

Q: Does the reason why the first man committed suicide matter?
A: No

Q: Is what the first man did for a living important?
A: Yes

Q: Did the second man try to call the first man's place of employment?
A: Yes

LANGUAGE SKILLS

Q: Does it matter what the native language of these individuals was?

A: Yes

Q: Could anyone read or write in the language of these individuals?

A: No

Q: Would it help to know what branch or division of the government employed these individuals?

A: Yes

IT'S ABOUT TIME

Q: If Reginald had placed the clock somewhere else in his study, would it have kept proper time?

A: No

Q: Would the clock have kept accurate time if it had stayed in the clock maker's shop?

A: Yes

Q: Does it matter what type of clock he purchased?

A: Yes

FAST FOOD

Q: Could Mike take his lunch break at any time of day?

A: No

Q: Does Mike take the same route home during his break that he uses on his way to and from work?

A: No

Q: Does Mike use a different mode of transportation to go home on his break?

A: Yes

THE LOVE NOTE

Q: Did Victoria neglect to search somewhere when she searched for the message earlier?

A: No

Q: Did Mark know that Victoria would not see the note until after she started to prepare for work?

A: Yes

Q: Did Mark use a pen or pencil to write the note?

A: No

STICKY FINGERS

Q: Did Joan rely on any form of surveillance to catch the criminal?

A: No

Q: Did Joan's plan provide her with visual evidence?

A: Yes

Q: Did Joan's plan rely exclusively on the contents of her lunch?

A: Yes

THE EVIDENCE

Q: Was Ken intentionally trying to help the mobster?

A: No

Q: If someone else had walked into the room, would the evidence have been destroyed?

A: Yes

Q: Did Ken know that walking into the room at the wrong time could destroy evidence?

A: Yes

Q: Is what type of room Ken walked into important?
A: Yes

CREATURE DISCOMFORT

Q: Did the animal do something that caused Bart to regret his actions?
A: Yes

Q: Did the animal physically injure Bart?
A: No

Q: If Bart had seen the animal beforehand, would he have thrown the rock?
A: No

An Alarming Change of Pace

Q: Does William cut in line because he's in a hurry?
A: No

Q: Does it matter what type of alarm William sets off?
A: Yes

Q: Does William need a co-worker in order to make a living?
A: Yes

Answers

An Alarming Change of Pace

William and his co-worker, Tim, are thieves. Their scam took place at an airport. William would cut in front of a traveler who had just placed an expensive-looking item on the x-ray conveyer belt. William would intentionally set off the metal detector a few times by failing to remove loose change and other items from his pockets. Meanwhile, Tim, who had already passed through the metal detector, would grab the expensive item and make his getaway.

The Alaskan Dream

Scott will need to travel to a hospital in order to have the battery replaced in his pacemaker within four years.

Attorney Client Privilege

Sam is visiting his lawyer, who had been arrested and jailed.

An Axe to Grind

The tree is a Japanese bonsai variety. Two-hundred-year-old bonsai trees typically grow only a few feet in height and a few inches in diameter.

Bad Medicine

Mel was suffering from amnesia. When he searched his pockets for a clue to his own identity, he found Dr. Greenwood's name and address written on a scrap of paper. He assumed that he had previously made an appointment with the doctor to help cure his amnesia. Although no appointment had been made, the kindly doctor helped Mel overcome his problem. When Mel was finally cured, he remembered that he had been hired as a hit man to kill Dr. Greenwood.

THE BIG GAME

The prominent citizen was the police chief. He called several of the city's most-wanted criminals, and claimed that they had won the tickets in a random drawing. When the criminals arrived to claim their tickets, they got more than they bargained for!

BILL'S BIRTHDAY SURPRISE

After hearing of an impending flood, Marion scrubbed her bathtub and filled it with water to be saved for drinking. Unaware that the city's water had already been shut off, Bill used the water to take a bath.

A BRIDGE TO FEAR

Patty was standing near one end of the bridge. She fell only a few feet to the ground.

BY THE TIME I GET TO PHOENIX

Nick knew that Frank would assume that he was referring to the West and East Coasts of America; however, he was thinking of a trip from the Atlantic Coast to the Gulf Coast of Florida. In fact, his trip took far less than the 24 hours he boasted about.

THE CINEMA SNEAK

Larry had managed to sneak into a movie that was being shown in 3-D. Larry lacked the necessary glasses required to get the full effect, so he left and returned later in the week.

CREATURE DISCOMFORT

Bart had the unfortunate luck to strike a skunk. The skunk promptly released a foul-smelling spray that ended up ruining his clothes.

CRUSTACEAN VACATION

As Milton launched the small boat they used to check the crab pots, he discovered a patch of dead grass where the boat had been resting. This indicated that the boat had not been moved for quite some time.

A CUSTOMS CONUNDRUM

Eric eventually died as a result of his skiing accident. His body was being flown home in the cargo section of a plane.

DEAD CONNECTION

The first man worked as the sole operator of a suicide hotline during the evening shift. When he received the news that his wife had just been killed in an automobile accident, he decided to end his own life. The second man was contemplating suicide and tried to call the suicide hotline. Getting no answer, and having nowhere else to turn, he took his own life as well.

DEAD MEN TELL NO TALES

The man was still alive when the search party found him. He

was able to tell the police the identity of his attacker. He later died at the hospital.

THE DEBATING CLUB

Each member of the group spoke only two languages, as follows:

> Sam speaks German and Spanish
> Jose speaks Spanish and French
> Pierre speaks French and English
> Joe speaks English and Japanese

The interruptions occurred when someone, acting as the interpreter, needed to consult a bilingual dictionary.

DIAMONDS ARE FOREVER

The man shook the box back and forth, knowing that the diamond would eventually wear a hole through the steel.

THE DISCOURAGING DISCOVERY

Vern had purchased his house for an exorbitant price with the understanding that the house had been constructed for W.C. Meadows, the famous movie star. In fact, the real estate agent had told him that W.C. Meadows had planted a sapling in the front yard when he first moved in. The storm had knocked over this very tree. While cutting up the tree, Vern counted the rings and discovered the tree was thirty years old. Unfortunately for Vern, W.C. Meadows had died *forty* years ago.

THE DOMINO EFFECT

The sugar was in the form of a cube, allowing Charlotte to pick up it by merely wetting her fingertip and touching its top.

DOWN ON THE FARM

Jedro's farm contained large hills, which increased its total surface area by 10%.

THE EVIDENCE

Ken was the custodian at a police station. The red warning light, mounted outside the police photo lab, was not lit and Ken assumed that it was safe to enter the room. By opening the door, he ruined the pictures that were in the process of being developed. The pictures showed Bebe Bologna, the infamous mobster, committing a heinous crime. Later, it was discovered that the warning light had merely burned out.

EXECUTION AT DAWN

When firing squads were used to carry out death sentences, a blank round was loaded into one of the guns used by the firing squad. This would allow each member of the firing squad to believe that he had not caused the prisoner's death.

THE EXPERT PILOT

The man was a Japanese kamikaze. Since he intended to crash his plane into an American battleship, he had no reason to be concerned with the faulty landing gear.

AN EXPLOSIVE SITUATION

The man worked for a traveling circus as a human cannonball.

EXPRESS CHECKOUT

Barry was purchasing milk and happened to notice the picture of the boy on the carton in his shopping basket. The caption stated that it was believed the boy had been abducted by his father. The strong resemblance between the boy and the adult convinced Barry to call the authorities.

EYES ON THE PRIZE

Alexander's name and credit cards were being used by an impostor ever since his wallet had been stolen. As he had not filled out a raffle ticket, when his name was announced as the winner he realized that the person impersonating him must have been present and filled one out. He simply waited around for the prize to be claimed in order to discover the identity of the culprit.

FAST FOOD

Mike's home was located on a small point of land at the mouth of a bay. His office was located on the opposite shore, a mere 300 yards away. On his way to and from work, Mike had to drive completely around the bay, a distance of sixty miles. Mike took his lunch break at low tide, at which time he could walk the short distance to his home.

FEAST OR FAMINE

Paul was a P.O.W. While incarcerated, his captors did not abide by the Geneva Convention rules concerning the treatment of prisoners of war. Paul refused to eat after realizing that he was being fattened up for his impending release.

FINDERS KEEPERS

Ted was working on a chain gang when he found the letter opener. He knew that he would be searched and the item confiscated before he was placed back in his prison cell.

A Fire Escape

Nicole was locked in a jail cell and realized it was futile for her to attempt to leave until the guard unlocked her cell door.

First Edition

Mr. Jones was a well known historian, and author of several books on the subject of World War II. He and his rival, Mr. Smith, had both recently published books on the Battle of the Bulge. He knew, happily, that his book would now seem so much the better in comparison.

The Frustrated Futures Trader

Over the weekend, Joe traded in his car for a vintage Jaguar which had its steering wheel on the right-hand side. The following Monday, he realized he would have to get out of his car every day on his way to work in order to pay the toll at the George Washington Bridge.

A Golden Opportunity

Bill's friend placed the bucket on a potter's wheel and activated it. Centrifugal force uncovered the coin, pushing the peas to the side of the bucket. It was then a simple matter to grab the coin from the center of the spinning bucket.

Hard of Darkness

To get a tan. For Ralph, who is an albino, this is impossible.

Harry the Homeowner

Harry had bought a doll house for his daughter. She had, of course, wasted no time in rearranging the furniture inside.

A Hunting Accident

Mick is a practitioner of falconry. One of his hunting falcons was sucked into the jet's intake and caused the engine to fail.

I Bid Thee Farewell

Dee works for a delivery service. The bid was delivered by a rival company. Taking offense to this, she discarded the bid without looking at it.

It's About Time

The study was located on Reginald's ship. The rolling motion of the waves caused the clock's pendulum to swing erratically, making the clock inaccurate.

Jury Duty

One of the jury members was deaf, and required an interpreter to help him communicate. The interpreter was the one person who had no vote.

Keep on Truckin'

Being a truck driver himself, Lewis knew that after many hours behind the wheel, his left arm would become more tan than other. In Australia vehicles are driven on the left-hand side of the road. Lewis saw that the truck drivers' right arms were heavily tanned and correctly surmised that they were from Australia.

The King's Test

The peasant left both buckets outside in freezing weather. Later that day, he took the now frozen blocks of water and milk out of the buckets, broke them into pieces and put them back into the buckets to yield an equal mixture of both.

LANGUAGE SKILLS

During WW II, the U.S. military tried to thwart enemy efforts to decode secret messages. They therefore employed Native American Navajo Indians. Their language has never been written down, and contains many subtleties, making it difficult to comprehend without actually having lived among them.

THE LEAKY BOAT

Al intentionally sank the boat knowing this would cause the wood to swell. This would seal the cracks in the hull.

LEAVE IT OR NOT

Elizabeth had moved in a few months before. For an upcoming art show, she decided to paint a 4-pane landscape of her house year 'round. Because it was only August, and she was a novice, she felt it would help her visualize the winter scene if she removed the leaves from her ornamental trees.

THE LETTER

Danielle feared being convicted of a felony crime. Since she possessed vital information that would clear her name, she sent the evidence to herself via registered mail. The date she received this evidence was crucial, so she left the letter intact.

THE LONG ROAD AHEAD

Bubba was a race car driver. Therefore he could see his destination, the finish line, at any moment during the race.

Long Time No See

Both the women had taken a vow of silence while living in a convent. It was only later, after having left the convent, that they were allowed to speak

The Love Note

Mark had written the note on the bathroom mirror with his finger, while it was still fogged up from the shower he had just taken. He knew that the condensation would soon evaporate. This left an invisible message for his wife which she would clearly see after having taken her shower.

Making the Grade

Alphonso was undergoing an eye examination required for entering the armed services. The examiner knew Alphonso had memorized the chart because the examiner had recently begun using a new chart and, unfortunately for Alphonso, he had memorized the outdated one.

The Master Mechanic

Gary had made a wager with Shawn that he could lie in the middle of a busy highway during rush hour for ten minutes. In order to safely win the bet, Gary drove Shawn's car to a near-by highway, feigned car trouble and climbed under the GTO. Ten minutes later he emerged five hundred dollars richer!

Money Troubles

The man was charged with embezzling large sums of money. In order to post his bond he would have to use the money he had embezzled. This would have strengthened the case against him.

MONUMENTAL ACHIEVEMENT

The monument the man had jumped off of was underwater. The whole town had been flooded years earlier, when a hydroelectric dam was built for a neighboring city.

MORE THAN HE BARGAINED FOR

While window shopping, Bert watched a news story about the grand opening of a new shopping center. Bert immediately recognized the site as the location where he had buried his accumulated wealth.

MOURNING GLORIA

Gloria was a lawyer who was looking for new clients. She hoped to approach the dead man's relatives in an attempt to bring a lawsuit against the drunk driver who had caused the victim's death.

MOVING DAY

Herb lives on a houseboat. While moving his houseboat, Herb causes a drawbridge to be raised, thereby blocking a major road.

MR. GRAY'S ANATOMY

Mr. Gray wants to have his head frozen once he is dead. He believes that, at some future time, technology will exist that will be able to bring the minds in frozen heads back to life.

THE MYSTERIOUS MOTORIST

Jennifer is a police officer. Opening the trunk partially disguises her patrol car from speeding motorists.

On the Boardwalk

Patrick deliveries helium balloons. The helium exerts a lifting force on the cart, thereby making it more difficult to push when empty.

Out of Bounds

The game was taking place in Cuba at the Guantánamo Bay Naval base. The ball was kicked over a fence into Cuban territory, making it dangerous to retrieve.

Peculiar Parking

Sam's religion requires him to have his head facing directly north while sleeping. In order to accomplish this, he must sometimes park his truck in more than one space.

The Perfect Crime

Rocky killed the person on the very day that an earthquake occurred. This made the person's death appear to be an accident caused by the natural disaster.

Petty Cash

Pauline is an avid coin collector. The five antique silver dollars were appraised at one thousand dollars.

The Phoned-in Message

Kathleen suspected her husband was staying at the hotel with another woman. Knowing the desk clerk would not divulge her husband's room number, she called from the lobby phone and watched to see in which box he placed the message.

PHOTO FINISHED

Ben had filmed his "week-long" vacation over the course of one day. On examining the tape, the police noticed that the phases of the moon did not change throughout the entire video. The moon would have changed significantly over a span of one week.

THE PILOT'S PUZZLE

The pilot was flying in a war zone. He had been instructed to look for grazing animals as an indication of a safe landing area. If land mines had been present, the animals would most likely have set them off as they grazed.

THE POEM

The man had been translating several poems from various languages into Spanish. While translating this one particular poem, he noticed that it rhymed. He therefore concluded, correctly, that it had been originally written in Spanish.

POTTED PLANTS

An alert employee at the local power company notified the authorities that Fred was using an exorbitant amount of electricity, as compared to his previous bills. The police soon suspected that this additional power was being used for illicit purposes.

THE PRISON BREAK

Jim was hired by the state authorities to test the security system at a new prison. He posed as a prisoner in order to attempt an escape. When he succeeded, the authorities were embarrassed by his accomplishment.

A Reverting Development

The storm caused a power line to be knocked down. Since the artist had been working on an ice sculpture in his refrigerated studio, he depended upon electric power to keep the work of art from melting.

Room Despair

The man was confined to a wheelchair. He wanted the extra room to accommodate visiting friends and relatives. The addition consisted of a second story on top of what had been a single-level home.

The Root of the Problem

Mr. Finkel accidentally cut his neighbor's phone line while planting the tree. His neighbor suffered a heart attack and was unable to call for help.

The Running Man

The man was a teammate who took a baton from Alex's hand during the course of a relay race.

The Secret Meeting

Their intimate conversations take place in a confessional. Therefore neither one can clearly see the other's face.

A Sense of Direction

B.J. was the architect who had designed the building. Knowing the layout of the building, she easily found her way to her destination.

Shed Some Light

The hermit's house was powered by photo-electric solar cells, which only operated in direct sunlight.

A Shooting at Midnight

The man shot his rooster, which had awakened him with its crowing every morning for the past ten years. Since he had recently retired, there was no longer any reason to be awakened at such an early hour.

Shore Sighted

The stranded group set off flares in the hope that those seeing them would come to their rescue. Unfortunately, the boat trip took place on a holiday, part of the reason for the outing, and the onlookers seeing the flares assumed that they were simply part of the firework displays that were part of the holiday celebrations.

Shortchanged

Minnie was traveling in Mexico when she received the tip. Unfortunately, all of the change she had in her pocket was still American currency. Minnie could not find anyone to exchange her money.

The Singing Kidnapper

Karl's speech was hindered by severe stuttering. Knowing that the police would attempt to trace the telephone calls he made, he realized that he needed to keep his messages as brief as possible. Instead of speaking, Karl therefore chose to sing his ransom demands, because he never stuttered while singing.

THE SKY DIVER

Unfortunately for Pierre, he did not survive the jump. However, his brother was in need of a transplant and was blessed enough to receive the necessary organ from an ideal donor.

THE SKY'S THE LIMIT

The treasure map relied on celestial navigation. Therefore Henry needed to wait until a specific date for a constellation to appear in the sky.

SOMETHING'S UP

When the man went to use the bathroom, he noticed that the toilet seat had been left up. The man had been "trained" by his wife to always lower the seat, but apparently her lover had not yet "learned" this lesson.

STICKY FINGERS

Joan vigorously shook the can of soda in her lunch bag. When the thief opened the can, he received a well-deserved shower of soda, which marked him as the perpetrator.

SWIMMING WITH THE FISHES

The man was ice fishing on a frozen lake. Unable to find the hole through which he had fallen, he consequently drowned.

TEMPORARY HOUSING

Jake had built a large tree house, which surrounded the main trunk. When the tree grows in diameter, the framing of the tree house will gradually be destroyed.

Theft in a Pub

J.P. was a counterfeiter. He left the wallet in plain view, knowing it was likely to be stolen, and the money spent. He then watched the transaction, thereby learning if the bogus money would pass as real currency without having to take the risk himself.

To Tell a Mockingbird

Christopher was a priest. In the confessional at church, John told the priest about his involvement in the crime. Christopher later learned of Bob's role while attending a church bake sale. Catholic priests are constrained from revealing information imparted to them in a confessional.

The Unsuccessful Suicide

The building was on fire at the same time the man tried to commit suicide, leading the police to believe he was only trying to save himself from the fire.

An Untimely Death

Cal was a coal miner and his pet, Roscoe, was a canary. In a bygone era, canaries were sometimes used to alert miners to the presence of flammable gases accumulating in the mines, which could cause a disastrous explosion. The small birds' low tolerance for gases would cause them to die, thereby warning the miners of the danger.

What's It All About?

Mack is a champion featherweight boxer. After his binge he was unable to make weight for his title bout.

WHOSE VAULT IS IT?

Using bubble gum, the thief disguised himself by blowing a large bubble, thereby concealing his face from the camera.

WONDER WOMAN

The woman was an astronaut aboard the Space Shuttle. In zero gravity conditions, large heavy objects can be easily manipulated.

WOOD THAT I COULD

Tom was expecting a boat to pass by the island on the tenth night. Since he had only enough wood for one fire, Tom waited until the boat was in sight. Coincidentally, this was the same night that it began to rain.

THE YARD SALE

Gerald is blind and fears he would be shortchanged by the purchaser. The bank teller would insure the proper amount is paid.

INDEX

Page key: puzzle, *clue*, **solution**